2.4.18

Dan Kaplan

the youngest luge Olympian in history.
Four years later, the Italian luge team offered
Keshavan full use of its world-class coaches and
facilities, an off-season job in the Italian police and
eventual citizenship if he agreed to compete under
their flag. Keshavan never even considered it. "For
me the dream was to get the Olympics to my home-

Winter is not a meaningful
seasonal category for nearly half the
world's countries.

town," he says. "And that was the only reason I was
doing it. To show that we are also here." Keshavan
has never won a medal in the Winter Olympics — no
Indian has. But he is the reigning Asian champion of
the sport, winner of 10 Asia Cup medals and hold-
er of the Asian speed record (83.5 miles per hour).
When he went home to India after winning his first
gold in the Asia Cup in 2005, "the entire town had
a holiday," he says. "They all carried me along the
main street, throwing flowers

Olympic Participant."
"There used to
newspaper like, 'We
Keshavan says. "Bu
pick anyb
the street, and with
turn them into a wo
don't have that ment
she says, "wa
on your own. They a
Olympic medal, e
won need fundin
In India the people w
any sport have been
their own lone journe
The Indian novelis
beautifully about the a
Indian Olympics fa
Keshavan. In pa
Olympics seems akin
fan before 2016: an al
heart-rending pathos
underdog (a sentimen
he noted, exploit to t
desire to recognize th

SPUYTEN DUYVIL

NEW YORK   PARIS

ISBN 978-1-959556-26-8

This book is an erasure of the February 4, 2018 issue
of *The New York Times*.

BRACES IN PLAY

Burns the warning sign,
it was their grip.

it was midwinter in exodus
where half opted
for a spacious border
grown favorable to fraying.

the landscape stirred
seats and machinery
enough to make inroads.

Matt said Walter said
"the energy is real."

That energy was red brick,
left open by breakfast
and multiplying.

EVERY ACT

blue coastal fields make more probable
a mildly surprising goose

that could pull up a widening margin.
when seeking weather to follow,

the pivot used up its slack, a net
effect clearer and larger than

a bump somewhere else, a light
boxed in by the painting itself.

the realities back away
from a good moment

when all ages can be stuck together
and one central peak built around.

ordered in thoughtful dimension
balloons form by the hundreds

to plug a leak in a ceiling—
the picture of some lonely outpost

unfolded, disordered
and rolled together.

last fall is still out there, live,
calm, incompatible with fact

and balance, cardinals disproportionate
to their actual numbers and appearance,

changing the location at least,
expanded yards and irises

in composite, small and perfected,
a kitchen smoking on the grounds,

sweeping other parts in circles and soft steps,
the children vibrant and shaky in a long line

hard to separate, the sketch narrowing,
clear sequence nudged ahead.

HOPING SOMEONE TOLD

to disappear in two-tone
and drop crotch capri pants
felt major

a child got into the toilets
and an alcove,
referring to the difficulties

There needs to be a place
where people misinterpret largely,
nestled in a crystal tree

sleep picked up
a frozen coin
out in the open

the wave was starting
at the house party

VISITORS ON A CLEAR DAY

a visitor can imagine spring,
the arcades discolored
and sun-roasted, some bread
and a mushroom, heavy and round,
birdsong a hole in the middle
where dampness came,
whispered and curled
atop a spare tire,
a table set with thick plates
and a chalky white bone.
I stuck a point in time
to a gum drop and other bits,
one mysterious form of faith
tucked against the other.

LIKELY SUBJECT

the pool is new
is so great at the beginning

the field shows at least
part of a plateau

the road shows some drifted leaves
their time has been found

all the lounges are active
the topics dominate those children

sleep returns to the rack
represents its inception

holding your hand would be better
far more painful

there may be evidence
of a bear

Up a day

Sometimes bodies.
Other times the snow brief,

two parrots printed in red ink
on the smoke.

Once it became clear

we returned skinny and young,
able to move,
asking for visitors.

the radioactively baked didn't come out
in the pretty town.
the hidden beginning flourished
and emptied an enormous rotunda rubbed in pastel.
an immense wild came down in a cool, dry month.
the low-flying plane chipped the narrative
which the butterflies would later describe.
the word sugar came for the candy-colored
and all that fantastic, the trees
dissolving into the trees.

REHEARSING FOR PEOPLE

standing barefoot
parts the language.

emotion is outsize,
the kind of primer

a love song roughly
doubled from the tumult.

it would not be

the first time
a line shrugged

and stumbled
from the stereo,

listening for
the others.

SHAVINGS

a face boils
it had a little beard
the following year

the significant factor
an interior big enough
to camouflage

little children
a patterned dress
anything but talking

I'm very good
at romantic
never disconnected

so is carbon
the stars on fire
a few cloudlike

New Walker

I'm all in the region
I'm on my way under
I'm functioning that poor checklist
I thought: that crumble
It's seriously good
There is no true attribute
If you leave
O.K. the fact to happen

Remotely I back winter
Ideally I am thinking
I lined up before a float
I pass many like that
a clean background

WOLF CATALOG

Jonathon watches the hills.

FIRST CLAIMS

people are tactile, yes

snow went into wide circulation

an authority would have gotten real

in little time, figures would matter

stirringly was not exactly wrong

alternately deemed affairs in prim illustration

your midst, which seemed clear

the gap was in view and on the ground

it was overrun

secret was how—it was that

a second can move casually, doing the informational

it is easy to tell the rest brightly

each morning, the incredibleness

things emerge from events

my little inventory becomes all horrified

jogging destroyed childhoods entirely

a small pressure sent ahead to the open slot

a supply of pleasant mints

I needed more face

the agreed to team

the sympathetic couldn't say extra

a workable plan was under pages I had

that part would be the only breakdown

fall had come in a handful, giving and getting

here at last was the long scheduled

daytime decided the errors and forms

it knows a good vacation

leaves were introduced on say-so

I have no interest in seeing a person

I understand animals and special bracelets

a kind radius found my disappearance

it's fancy as an afterthought

it affects the presence of the inside

precise and glassy

the soft extra will emerge

the margin will absorb the center position

the so-called exception may be identical

I never saw in detail entire shinbones

there is really only one way to achieve this

everyone must carry the same same

all aspects—little room, single mechanism, complete nature

pond in the middle of a longer note

re-emerging—knees and shoulders, eyes

smooth experience pressures an exit

the chaperones were qualified and tidy

days had bad materials

no specific field was searching for them

meaningful was only flowers

meaningful a train suspended from the opening

the first will need attention, and more consecutive

a trait was explaining leg strength and rehearsing stylishly

the short pool was endless with spectacles

what is watchable for schoolchildren

largely, the shadows slide over the old-growth

great consolations: these people

they can be plenty

the trees considered the soundness

whalebone, butterfly, horsehair

the superlight articulated outward

they charmed the unnatural

to feel it happen is exactly that

to resemble the geometry of a wing

the early movements show grace

the mussed in a brighter light

it involves more than counting on an unsteady surface

I can do something

I don't really like the lifeless holding a hose

the pebbles slide from the quarries

they stand up close to the frozen bogs in modern form

clouds

the chief appeal may lie crushed or unscarred

I got up for the No. 1 warning

you haven't seen it popular

the fact is essentially romantic

the whole feeling explains its interior

my body found me

I apologize in a costume of bubbles

the minute one

the row of tiny, bad children—

eat fruit, do little jumps

I stand there with my eyes closed

I visualize a complex

the high points are contained and distressed

a lovely sequence will be the first white clouds

OFFERS

to add fully
is likely designed
to reduce a second

to repeat
to be unclear often
appears rare

to be in California

to order part
of a sentence,
only one
in each chapter

to move
the desk

SMOOTH GETTING

the most exciting days line up exactly in this
exact situation—blue and green gradually turning
something not part of either. I've never had
long conversations while walking around a goodbye
or easy names like Golden 500 worth having for accuracy,
sometimes a pin or something to drop it in.

ACCESSORY OF DETAIL

winter approaches costume—

wings, panels, Beltline
to expand the most open stretch of interior landscape

branches, color effects,
animals from elsewhere

PEAR FOUND

information is vague.

nature forms detailed,
dressing in the light.

IN FROM AND

fruit can be remarkable,
curling up
the surroundings
of the central environment,

a piece torn across
the either or.

not always so
were the millions
so a few sprung
the picturesque:

viewpoints and bears
in the original language

and a flagship
for the flood.

no one seems to know
the big happening,
hanging black curtains
in all the windows.

In Some Ways Special

A showcase of perceptions
has not stopped a number.

Being is the starting point
wherever vision singles out,

is looser and more dispersed,
can measure new attention

for the latest named.
We are hopeful this is

a way. We made that
in highlights amid the works

like a showpiece of concrete
to hang on in the fields.

DRAWINGS FOR THE BOX

The personal grace came from pleasures I don't understand very well

There's a reflection of every experience

Surprisingly, I don't like cold cream while high

10 leaves usually arrive

Also a pancake

The special person

Pick that person to speak to

DID NOT CHOOSE

the late one
ended last

because the next
was not well understood.

the long-term started,
the effects countless

in a dollhouse,
brush and dishes

arranged
for living,

time visibly shocked
like a movie character

with one hand
on a ghost.

THE MOST DRAMATIC YET

the scenes have grown
closer on both sides…

then a change
solidified both sides…

the wave briefly retreated
and the wave appeared
to follow the former—

an open lid
is open widely enough
out of goodness…

for example…

WARM EFFECT

hundreds of stars barely
get to scale

each day could become
the most bright green

gloomy was rejected
and describing it easy

I have several friends
and get the same effect

home
with small canopy

LIGHT COVER

canopies suggested more
we knew there was more

a television special
lost in the television

a spot in the landscape
also a sea in the field

10

I was like
oh my God
I want plotters for dreaming,
a dragon flashing
on a live background.

You know, half supports that—
nature coming up the door,
days on the face.
The end, don't feel sad,
means last.

Fantasy with skippy

These doublets
and the flecks of fake blood.
The Dutch,
the 1970s,
a wet suit
you can cut off.
And a plain pastoral,
everyone appears in yellow,
the coffins dance,
the cat in bandages,
these funny little shoulders
of the oldest white horse.

JUICE FORWARD

someone like me has an effect
on my day—

pouty and played,
waking up a stone.

the Cod have yellowed,
it makes me spit,

and, more miraculous,

extravaganza,
the Olympics.

TWO CENTERS

And the leaves deliver
badly needed reaction,
spinning the source
of the noise.

The end softened
against the thought
returning longer,
but only then.

BIG TIME

many see the spreadsheet—
another example of and.

Here there can exist a convergence
of the number and the number

eliminated altogether,
a confounding place,

a second sentence
popping from the same period,

a subject that revolves
a record almost perfectly

despite the changing actors
and their good intentions.

Worst details

realistic with blue is very very

the environment
the response to the commonplace lights

a window can play first person
can also play a realistic person
active in the spring

a fly does not always transfer the same fidelity
it's possible to live in a basic field of wow
to run the exact order

So In

the past
a few weeks

each year,
cracked open
in the snowfall

APPLAUDING

Blinder from the outside
I like the biggest purple
around the unromantic view.

You've got to have a collection
of big Lakes
and a seat there, a swing
a cloud brings up.

BIG CHALLENGES

My figure detailed in this very area
The greater use of alternatives to these areas
One mercifully copies that project
The sad water impossible to place
The right set of intricate structures
Representative of a premier drama
fit for crazy watching
The wing a sign most dangerous itself
One which divided the view by expanding it
Why this doesn't mean hinterlands
filled with people and all the leaves

FIRST APPLIED

to wave hardly
seemed promising,

a mountain and snow
which never stopped dancing.

it used to take Moon-thought,
spelled with the capital.

time will change that,
bristling in the hills

and the happiest thing.

FAST TALLY

The big children were big.

Holding everything -

a net, a Crow,
some sentences,
a hand -

is big.

That may change
one day.

Room for space

a highly desirable quality refers to undesirable something else

all those songs about little pockets
stay in that pocket in your face

sudden is actually a plus and a subsequent

who can explain such things in sweatpants
with extra responsibilities

same line with rental dog

TO TELL THE GLAMOROUS

to plan
is a new explosion
on the lovelorn.

to punish
an enormous image
of honey.

every day said this
and offered a star.

to generate
a form far
less artificial

is my favorite part,
the way it was up again
and staying.

LIKE I'M OUTSIDE

me time will be a fraction of the static

it traces small friends in a large book

wearing a bucket is insane for a well-lit public wave

the most openness won't find the body that oversees it

occasional exceptions…

what's called a "show" place—

more stars, a great snowstorm

CALLED ONLY

the doors are tasteless.
the wave is sour, emerging opposite,

a skirt doubles around the hands.

now sounds quite early,

low-focused, everybody has this,
suited and still

pouring open.

CARDINALS YOU DON'T REMEMBER

The most cradled never came,
tying reasonable minds into the erased.
Moss endured untouched in the memory
of luminous history. That was the time
to prevent the worst circumstances,
to foresee the deep middle left open.
Cardinals sailed through the lost field
and the last home watching it.
Feeling needed a receiver
after a kite did not appear
and slipped free.

The odds of precise situation—
I hate a neat Nothing.
It was reaction:
left groin, then right,
my eyes closed
on two different states:
spectacular and jammed,
shining down and draped
over a single line.
The overshadowed half
would remember the covering
and later fade into the same day.

When illuminating
a small sack of numbers,
the exact saturates every layer.
The model
drawing hundreds of simulations
tends purely unblemished.
Not so much in their frequency,
the weeks increased something
they're giving away.
It can be overwhelming.
It seemed natural.

Still fans kept the wind.
Fine sounds like fabric
adhere to motion
from the center,
adding details
with little hold…
this covered yard
is a version of ending.
But that dog appeared.

If you remove the overall
one seems closer.
The embraced
favored a newer outfit
and it's definitely last season.
The stars expose
their growing number
on a string,
learning the remarkable.

Before another figure
walked toward a feeling
a cat played everywhere.
Things could change,
pry a few words loose
when they became clear,
close to possible,
an index of flair
and sparkling form.
Real happy
was difficult to regain
after fragile.

If better suits work
this might prove magical.
I admired sudden
before halfway,
was becoming at times.
Obviously it's something
of a moment I can only
imagine in flurries,
across the highs
and the very highs.

Look happy

balloon

THE CLEAREST HAVE DOGS AND COWS AND CHICKENS

the days flinched quietly, contemplating better this time

I promised to take lessons

I remained with no interior flock

the afternoons seemed moving, which meant bigger worries

a child searching lightly also stayed buoyant

the music got tiny

BAKER DAYS

pronouncing fire
is unlike anything,
folks sought the hidden hand
in a deep nest.
I think of another time

this happened,
a bear reporting
his own actions,
an apparatus
tied to a few actors.
What is greater,

how people think
in a field of glass
under a cloud.

FRIENDS BE FRIENDS

it feels ugly so it matters more—

about 40 percent more,

the amounts are relatively small,
can be substantial,

that makes it easier to smile however,

I'm sure it's different,
has always been soft,

there is no longer the special question

what does this mean for Belgium?

Not together

the fact naturally ended up
in a roped-off section

it was weird
to be onetime
in more ways than one

to be prefigured
in a negative

every little star
huge and biological
operating in common

EASIER TO WEAR

from the house's sleeker side
a long match in winter
can give a sense of ease

the highlights belonged
to the picturesque

I picked up a side

underneath was something

those children
these chairs

remind me to cycle by
the most intense pink

In House

a clear form ballooning to new shape, loosening
the expression of summer, the associated pool viewed
as somewhat broader, the rise over a select city unlikely
to set an effect across the spectrum beyond slow spread

some flies on a figure
small, private, shy

By Daniel

scenic,
inflatable

history
without history

FROM INSIDE

Early devolved
by the end,

was many
multiples,
included

a different red.

The next day released
counterparts
to the backgrounds,

details tiny
inside the motion.

MATTER RISEN

expiring in the Bay completed the extra.

to behave overwhelmingly can be costly
to the clear faced.

this mistake,
to imagine error in the unrelated,

how the future was, was likely
the same.

WELCOMES FROM THE SOFT

sound has a favorite corner
has been working the backyard
the plants the forests
in thin strips of contrast
the slightly rough texture especially
the given features
dazzling for grander atmosphere
an exact replica
wasn't easy to communicate
had been a demonstration of interiors
that survived the shiny and fine
not a bad thing
not to find a radiant garden

CONTINUED FROM PAGE 1

20 miles southwest. In June 2014, ISIS overran it and the group's leader, Abu Bakr al-Baghdadi, stood inside its Great Mosque of al-Nuri and named himself caliph of the terrifying regime. By August 2014, ISIS' ominous black flags snapped just three miles from where I now stood. Under the cover of night, the monastery's manager, a priest named Yousif Ibrahim, whose brother had already been murdered by the militants, spirited away scores of ancient documents, the last of the monastery's once magnificent library, and even a discolored handbone fragment believed to have belonged to St. Matthew the Hermit, who founded the monastery in 363 A.D. He was certain the monastery would be lost. But then the airstrikes began and the Kurdish Peshmerga and Iraqi Army turned the tide on the ground. The caliphate began to crumble.

It was now May 2017 and most of the artifacts had been returned to the monastery. This was one of the first times that Mr. Schute had brought travelers here since ISIS had come so close. Today Mr. Schute believes that Kurdistan could be one of the world's great travel destinations if people would only stop confusing it with the Iraq they see in the news.

To be sure, Kurdistan is nothing like the Iraq of Mosul but a Middle Eastern Montana with ruins: a cooler, welcoming tableau of crisp mountain streams and scrappy peaks. A traveler can ski at a new resort serviced by gondolas or wander through the sun-roasted walls of the deepest canyon in the Middle East. You can drink city water from the taps and stroll around Erbil, the regional capital, concerned with only how to decline, politely, invitations to drink tea.

"Hello, my friend, have some bread."

"Come, sit."

"Please, mister, enjoy my country."

For now, the war with ISIS was still winding down. Soon we would watch a 500-pound coalition bomb erupt over the militants' last stronghold in Mosul and seen a huge mushroom cloud curling over the city. The concussion, heavy and round, would ring for miles. Here at the monastery, though, on this pleasant spring day, bird-song ricocheted off the cliffs and the only things to explode were the poppies.

As a West Point history major with a soft spot for heavy metal, Mr. Schute had been a state trooper in New Jersey before being called to Iraq in April 2003 to command a United States Army Reserve civil affairs battalion. "Those are the guys who help get people and things out of the way so the Army can come in and break stuff," he said.

TIM NEVILLE *is a frequent contributor to the Travel section.*

Soon he became something of a celebrity as the senior American officer in Kurdistan. To this day the Kurds, who view Americans as their liberators for ousting Saddam Hussein, recognize him on the street and ask for photographs with him. As his tour drew to a close, Mr. Schute began to feel anxious.

"It was like there was a hole in me," he said. "I felt I was in the middle of contributing worthwhile things and I wanted to continue to contribute. I wanted to stay."

The Kurdistan Regional Government eventually offered him a job in Erbil, about 225 miles north of Baghdad. For a history buff, Kurdistan was a dream. He could hear swords ringing on grassy fields where ancient armies collided. He ran his hands along the ramparts of forgotten fortresses and felt the dampness in the crypt-like passages of mystical shrines. He learned Kurdish and married a Kurd.

In 2003 at a Kurdish investment seminar in Erbil, Mr. Schute met Douglas Layton, an American who came to Kurdistan in 1990. Mr. Layton, whose round spectacles and woolen cap lend him the air of a paperback spy, had survived a $1 million bounty on his head, courtesy of Hussein. After the dictator's capture and execution, Mr. Layton journeyed to Hussein's palace in Baghdad, where he found his outlandish throne and sat in it. "You're gone," Mr. Layton whispered to Hussein's ghost, "and I'm still here."

Mr. Schute and Mr. Layton, who had been working for the Meridian Health Foundation, both knew of Kurdistan's cultural riches and friendly people, so they joined forces to create what eventually became Kurdistan Iraq Tours, the only inbound tourism operator in Kurdistan. The idea seemed absurd.

"Everyone said no one will come to Iraq, and I said but they'll come to 'the other Iraq'!" Mr. Layton recalled. "I believed, and I still believe, that tourism is the future."

For their main local guide, they hired and trained Balin Zrar, a charismatic, chain-smoking Kurd. Mr. Zrar had spent seven years running an Italian restaurant in London after he smuggled himself to Europe — an epic tale that involved time in a Belgian prison camp and riding for days curled atop a spare tire under a tractor-trailer. After the London bombings, Mr. Zrar returned to Kurdistan to dabble in real estate. For the guide position interview, Mr. Layton asked him if he liked history. "I hate history," said Mr. Zrar, now in his early 40s, and the candor landed him the job: no one believed he would be busy.

In 2008, though, things took off. The company landed a contract with California-based Distant Horizons to run its Kurdistan cultural trips and soon others followed. Momentum built. By 2011 The New York Times

scout for the International Luge Federation.

Luge is one of three Olympic sled sports (it's the one in which the racer lies fully exposed, faceup and feet first) and it has always been dominated by Germany, Austria and Italy. But if the sport was to remain in the Olympics, it needed to field athletes from more countries, so Lemmerer was searching for them all over the warmer world. He picked Keshavan to join a luge training camp, which began with a film screening of Olympic luge highlights, complete with dramatic crashes, followed by "Cool Runnings," the 1993 Disney movie about the Jamaican bobsled team. "I was very inspired by it," Keshavan says. The next year Lemmerer took him to his first race, in Austria. Keshavan promptly broke his foot — and scored a good enough time that Lemmerer thought he could qualify for the Olympics the following year. And then there he was, all alone in Nagano, Japan, the only Indian in the 1998 Games, the only Indian ever to qualify for luge and, at 16, the youngest luge Olympian in history.

Four years later, the Italian luge team offered Keshavan full use of its world-class coaches and facilities, an off-season job in the Italian police and eventual citizenship if he agreed to compete under their flag. Keshavan never even considered it. "For me the dream was to get the Olympics to my home.

Winter is not a meaningful seasonal category for nearly half the world's countries.

town," he says. "And that was the only reason I was doing it. To show that we are also here." Keshavan has never won a medal in the Winter Olympics — no Indian has. But he is the reigning Asian champion of the sport, winner of 10 Asia Cup medals and holder of the Asian speed record (83.5 miles per hour). When he went home to India after winning his first gold in the Asia Cup in 2005, "the entire town had a holiday," he says. "They all carried me along the main street, throwing flowers."

In theory, the Winter Olympics is a global event. But winter is not a meaningful seasonal category for nearly half the world's countries. And nearly half of the countries of the world have never competed in the Winter Games. Of the 22 Winter Olympics, India has sent athletes to only nine, at two of them represented by a team consisting only of Shiva Keshavan.

Without institutional support, Winter Olympians from the so-called smaller nations have to hustle year round just to train. This year, one Jamaican bobsledder is literally having a bake sale, peddling banana bread to raise funds. In the off-season, Keshavan works as a waiter and pizza chef in the Italian restaurant his parents run near their Himalayan town. He has had few sponsors, and only since 2008, when Coca-Cola first paid him to carry around a branded bottle for the season. Otherwise, like many of his equatorial peers, he crowdfunds online. "It's awkward," he says. "But it has to be done."

Indian Olympic Association, and he practically did a spit take. "In 20 years, the Indian Olympic Association hasn't given me a dime," he said, laughing. Two months ago he emptied his bank account and maxed out his credit card to keep touring coaches, and only because the Indian government's ministry of sports agreed at the last minute to cover $8,000 of his debt. He had been fruitlessly petitioning them for help for five years. Once, he said, "they actually asked me to get a certificate to prove that Winter Olympics is similar with Summer Olympics."

India, the second-most-populous country in the world, is at the absolute worst at the Olympics in general, with the lowest number of medals per capita. Indian Olympic officials sometimes seem determined to embarrass their country's athletes. Two years before the 2014 Games, the Indian Olympic Association was suspended from the Games over a corruption controversy, and Keshavan had to walk the opening ceremony as an "Independent Olympic Participant."

"There used to be all these ridiculous stories in the newspaper like, 'We are genetically not suited,'" Keshavan says. "But anybody can do it. I think you could pick anybody with some aptitude from the street, and within eight to 10 years you can turn them into a world-class athlete. But still we don't have that mentality in India," Indian sports officers, he says, "want you to first win something on your own. They actually tell me, You win an Olympic medal, and then we'll help. At that point I won't need your funding! But that's the way it's been. In India the people who have brought attention to any sport have been individuals who have gone on their own lone journey."

The Indian novelist Amitava Kumar has written beautifully about the agony and ecstasy of being an Indian Olympics fan. I called him to ask about Keshavan. In part, Kumar's love of India at the Olympics seems akin to that of a Chicago Cubs fan before 2016: an almost masochistic revel in the heart-rending pathos of the perennial tournament underdog (a sentiment that Bollywood sports films, he noted, exploit to the maximum). But it's also a desire to recognize the genuine achievement even of those who never medal. He raved about Dipa Karmakar, who became the first female Indian Olympian gymnast despite having only minimal gymnastics facilities in her hometown, and who is known for performing a vault so dangerous that American Olympians often attempt it. And he recalled watching the live counting performance in women's badminton of P.V. Sindhu as "an extraordinary experience — not least because my daughter said, 'Dad, I'd love to play badminton.' My God. Look at what a transformative electric effect P.V. Sindhu has on other Indians — especially other Indian women."

But Keshavan's lonely luge mission, he said, while clearly impressive, "has that quixotic element to it which makes him more in line with another phenomenon — which is of Indians entering the Guinness Book of World Records in vast numbers." As in, most consecutive armpit positions (Continued on Page 79)

((NOTES AND ACKNOWLEDGMENTS))

The rule I followed in the writing of this book: the emerged text must appear in the order in which I encountered it in the physical paper.

Thank you, journalists, for the work you do.

Thanks, tt and Aurelia.

Susie and Stella: thanks thanks love love love.

Dan Kaplan is the author of *2.4.18* (Spuyten Duyvil, 2023), an erasure of the February 4, 2018 issue of *The New York Times*; *Instant Killer Wig* (Spuyten Duyvil, 2018); *Bill's Formal Complaint* (The National Poetry Review Press, 2008); and the bilingual chapbook *SKIN* (Red Hydra Press, 2005). His work has appeared in *American Letters & Commentary*, *VOLT*, *Denver Quarterly*, *Ninth Letter*, *Poetry Northwest*, the anthology *Flash Fiction Forward* (W. W. Norton & Co.), and elsewhere. He is editor of Burnside Review Press and lives in Portland, Oregon.